PORTRAIT OF
ARMAGH

DARREN McLOUGHLIN

HALSGROVE

First published in Great Britain in 2009

British Library Cataloguing-in-Publication Data
A CIP record for this title is available from the British Library

ISBN 978 1 84114 971 4

HALSGROVE
Halsgrove House,
Ryelands Industrial Estate,
Bagley Road, Wellington, Somerset TA21 9PZ
Tel: 01823 653777   Fax: 01823 216796
email: sales@halsgrove.com

Part of the Halsgrove group of companies
Information on all Halsgrove titles is available at: www.halsgrove.com

Printed and bound by Grafiche Flaminia, Italy

INTRODUCTION

At 484 sq. miles Armagh is the smallest of Northern Ireland's counties. The compact size makes it perfect for touring around and enables the visitor to see the full range of landscapes and attractions in the county. Packing in a lot from the rugged geological landscape of Slieve Gullion in the south of the county, to the fertile apple growing north the area is rich in natural and cultural attractions.

The name Armagh comes from *Ard Mhacha* which means Macha's Height, referring to the goddess Macha who features prominently in Ulster Cycle mythology.

Armagh has an important place in Irish mythology and history, as a result of which St Patrick chose one of its hills on which to build his principal church in Ireland in 445 AD. After St Patrick decreed that only those who were educated in Armagh could teach the gospels, it became the ecclesiastical capital and centre of learning. To this day Armagh has two cathedrals dedicated to the patron saint, and is the smallest city in Ireland. It also has some of the finest Georgian architecture outside of Dublin.

Another of its many monikers 'The Orchard County' refers to Armagh's position as the apple growing centre of Ireland. Centred on the north of the county around Loughgall, the principal apple is the Bramley which is used for cooking and juice making. There is some evidence of the presence of apples here dating back 3000 years, and there are references to St Patrick planting apple trees in Armagh. During May the apple blossom is out and the hillsides are blanketed in thousands of trees bearing pink and white flowers.

Not being indigenous to Armagh, but having lived here for over fifteen years gives me the ability to see it from the viewpoint of both outsider and local. Picking up on the small things that local inhabitants miss while in the course of their daily lives, I know where to head off the beaten path and find the landscapes that visitors hurry past on their way to the star attractions.

During the course of making this book I have had some great experiences with the people of County Armagh, their friendly, welcoming nature making photography much easier. Unfortunately the same cannot be said of cattle that on many occasions had me outnumbered in the corner of a field.

I hope this book inspires locals and visitors alike to enjoy, as I have, travelling around this county of contrasts.

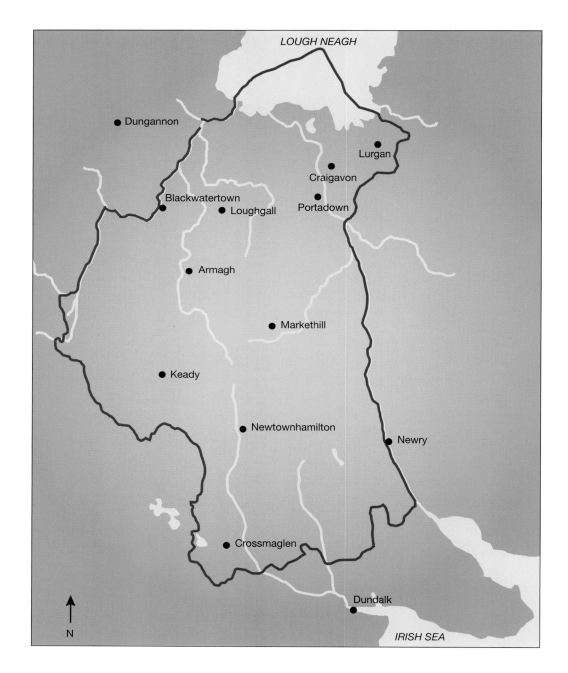

Jetty, Lough Neagh
Remains of a jetty on Lough Neagh – the largest lake in Ireland and Britain.

Snowy Farmstead
Situated on the slopes of Slieve Gullion, this isolated farmstead is exposed to severe winter weather.

Ponies in the Snow
Ponies such as these can be seen throughout the south of County Armagh.

Navan Fort
Emain Macha in Irish, an important site in Irish history and mythology. Human activity can
be found dating from c.4000 BC but the central mound dates to 95 BC.

Right: **Mourne Mountains**
View of the Mourne Mountains as seen from Carn Hill. The Mournes, situated in Co. Down,
inspired C.S. Lewis's land of Narnia.

Road, South Armagh
A snow-covered road in South Armagh. Snow rarely lies for more than three days due to the mild climate.

Reflections in a Lake
A typical winter lake with reflections on a calm day.

Darkley
The village of Darkley, a centre of linen production from the mid-eighteenth century to the mid-twentieth century.

Kilnasaggart Stone Pillar
8ft high, this pillar dates from 700 AD
and is the oldest dateable Christian
stone monument in Ireland.

Tynan High Cross
This Celtic High Cross is a
reconstruction from various
fragments but dates to the eighth
century; like many high crosses
in Ireland the originals were
destroyed over the centuries.

Left: **Tynan Abbey Gate Lodge**
Dating from 1817 this gate lodge
has been attributed to the architect
John Nash. The house to which it
relates no longer stands.

Sheep in a Snowy Field
Winter scene in South Armagh.

The King's Stables
There is a man-made pool here dating from 1000 BC. Legend has it that the Kings of Ulster watered their
horses and washed their chariots here. Archaeological finds here include the facial part of a
human skull, which suggests the site was used for ritual purposes.

Armagh Franciscan Friary
Founded in 1263, this was Ireland's longest medieval friary
church. Dissolved in 1542 and ruinous by 1600.

Right: **Ballymacdermot**
Winter as seen from Ballymacdermot court tomb. Dating from
around 3500 BC, this cairn is impressively situated on the edge
of a steep slope with sweeping views over Meigh.

Clady Milltown
One of many remnants of the industrial past, Clady Milltown is named for this mill.

Right: **Horses**
Photographed close to Crossmaglen, an area known for horse breeding.

Looking South from Victoria Lock
In the distance can be seen the Cooley Mountains, in Co. Louth which borders Co. Armagh.

Victoria Lock
The sea entrance to the redesigned Newry Ship Canal, completed in 1850. Designed by Sir John Rennie, the engineer responsible for London Bridge.

Albert Basin, Newry
Newry is chiefly in Co. Down but a small portion is in Co. Armagh. The Newry Canal was the first summit level canal in Ireland or Britain and opened for traffic in 1742.

Bessbrook

Founded by John Richardson in 1845 as a model village. The Richardsons were a Quaker family who were in the linen business. The village was envisaged to have no pubs, no pawn shops and no police. To this day there is still no pub for the 3000 inhabitants.

Right: **Schoolhouse, Bessbrook**
Originally from 1853 but enlarged in 1875.

Slieve Gullion
Sliabh Cuilinn in Irish. The highest point in Armagh at 573m, the mountain is the
weathered remains of an extinct volcano formed some 60 million years ago.

Moyry Castle Landscape
Built in 1601 by Lord Mountjoy to defend the Gap of the North, a pass
which took the main south-north route at the time.

Armagh Cathedrals
View of Armagh as seen from the southwest, with both cathedrals dominating the skyline.

Forkhill
Foirceal in Irish, this village lies in South Armagh in the shadow of Slieve Gullion. It had 366 inhabitants in the 2001 census.

Statue of Archbishop Daniel MacGettigan

Primate of the Roman Catholic Church in Ireland (1870-1887). MacGettigan oversaw the building of
the cathedral, taking over from Archbishop Crolly who began the work in 1838.

View of St Patrick's Roman Catholic Cathedral
Originally designed and started in the English Perpendicular Gothic style, building was interrupted by the Great
Famine in 1844. A new architect was appointed in 1854 who chose to continue in the French Decorated Gothic style.

Interior of the Roman Catholic Cathedral
Traditional cardinals' hats can be seen suspended from the ceiling.

Detail of the Ceiling of the Roman Catholic Cathedral
The vaulted ceiling of St Patrick's Cathedral.

Right: **Mosaic**
Mosaics cover every inch of the floor and walls of St Patrick's Roman Catholic Cathedral.

Right: **Armagh Streetscape**
The medieval street pattern can be seen centred
on the Church of Ireland Cathedral.

Door
Doorway of St Patrick's Roman Catholic Cathedral.

Post Office Red
Royal Mail postbox outside
St Patrick's Church of
Ireland Cathedral.

Vicar's Hill
Built in 1724 as accommodation for clergy widows. As seen from the
grounds of St Patrick's Church of Ireland Cathedral.

39

Nuadha
This statue is known as Tandragee
Man. After losing his arm in battle,
Nuadha had a silver arm made so that
he could become a physically perfect
King of Ireland.

Left: **Interior of the
Church of Ireland Cathedral**
Here, in 445 AD St Patrick established
his principal church. The general
layout is based on the thirteenth
century cathedral, but most of what is
visible dates from 1834.

St Patrick
Stained glass representation
of St Patrick.

Left: **Cathedral Steps**
One of the oldest sections
of the cathedral.

ST PATRICK

The Courthouse, Armagh
Built in 1809 the courthouse sits at the northern end of the Mall. Designed by the architect Francis Johnston.

Charlemont Place
A five house terrace built from 1827. Regarded as the finest Georgian terrace in Ireland, outside of Dublin.

Right: **Georgian Door**
Detail of a Georgian door on the Mall, Armagh.

Castle St., Armagh
Castle Street was built in 1773 and sits adjacent to the Church of Ireland Cathedral.

View of St Patrick's Cathedral
The Church of Ireland Cathedral seen from the grounds of the Observatory.

Marketplace Square, Armagh
This is a modern replica of an eleventh century cross which stood here, the civic centre of Armagh.

Armagh Observatory
Early morning sunlight hits the Observatory building, the last of Archbishop Robinson's public works.
Built to Francis Johnston's designs it was completed in 1793.

49

Armagh Observatory
These circular and square
towers were later additions
in 1827 and 1841.

Armagh Observatory
Telescopes at the Observatory, which remains one of the leading scientific research establishments in Ireland or Britain.

The Hill of Infinity
Situated in the Armagh Astropark. Every 10 metres up the hill represents a tenfold increase in distance from the Sun with markers placed to show significant universal phenomena.

Archbishop Robinson's Chapel
In the form of a Greek temple, designed for Archbishop Robinson in 1781
by Thomas Cooley and completed by Francis Johnston.

Right: **Chapel Interior**
Interior as seen from the musicians' gallery. The Primate's throne sits to the right, opposite which is a fireplace.

Armagh Public Library
The public library holds an extensive collection of rare books including a first edition of
Gulliver's Travels by Jonathan Swift, annotated by the author.

Right: **Armagh Public Library**
Bust of Archbishop Richard Robinson in Armagh Public Library. Built to designs by Thomas Cooley in 1771,
Archbishop Robinson spent £3000 on this building which was constituted by an Act of Parliament in 1773.

Armagh Public Library
The spiral staircase.

Marketplace Theatre
The theatre attracts top musicians from all genres, comedians and visual artists both local and international.

Bluebells

Hyacinthoides non-scripta or Cloigín Gorm in Irish. Here seen growing in typical Irish habitat. May is the month for Bluebells, and many of the woods and forests in Ireland are carpeted with this fantastic blue and green.

Bluebells
Woodland with path through bluebells. Bluebells are a protected species
under The Wildlife (Northern Ireland) Order 1985.

Orchard
These old apple trees have a surreal feel on an overcast day. Bramley apples grow well on the silt loam soils in the region, and form the majority of apples grown in the county. By 1921 over 7000 acres were planted.

Left: **Classic Tractors**
Classic tractor events are a common scene during spring and summer.

Apple Blossom
White apple blossom of eating apples,
not so common in the county.

Orchard
Bramley apples contain a higher acid content and lower
sugar levels than other varieties thus producing a stronger
tasting apple whose flavour is retained when cooked.
Because of this, the apple pies and tarts made with
Bramleys are far superior to any other.

Bramley Apple Blossom
Bramley apple blossom lasts for about
ten days in early May.

Orchard

Armagh is known as the Orchard County, and with good reason. Travelling the back roads in the centre and north of the county it is hard to imagine that anything else is grown here, every hillside is covered almost exclusively with rows of Bramley apples – *Malus domestica* 'Bramley's Seedling' – giving a landscape unique in Ireland.

Laneway
Typical rural laneway,
found all over the
county.

64

Laneway
Typical rural laneway
with May blossom
falling.

65

Ramsons – *Allium Ursinum*
Creamh in Irish. This widespread plant carpets woodland
and damp hedgerows in April and May, adding a
garlic fragrance to the air.

Right: **Ancient Remains**
Archaeological remains with Slieve Gullion in the background.

Cashel Hill
Giving spectacular views in all directions, the cashel has a diameter of 130ft. The wall has been depleted for building
material during the past century. The largest piece of amber found in Ireland came from here.

Tandragee Castle after the Storm

Begun in 1830 for Lord Mandeville who later became 6th Duke of Manchester. It became too expensive to run and stood empty from 1925. Since 1955 it has been the site of the world-renowned Tayto Crisp factory.

Geese
Geese in Lurgan Park, Northern Ireland's largest public park.

Lurgan Lion
Lion on Coalbrookdale fountain in Lurgan Park, one of the few surviving examples.

Crabtree Cottage
Situated close to Portadown, this cottage dates from the early eighteenth century.

Crabtree Cottage
There is a bow in the central portion of the cottage, seen here. Recently re-thatched.

Hawthorn
Hawthorn blossom turns the hedgerows white during May.

Right: **Cusher Bridge, Clare**
Seventeenth-century bridge with pedestrian
refuges notable on either side.

74

Graveyard
Remains of a church in Loughgall.

Left: **Graveyard**
Old graveyards abound in Armagh.

Mowhan
Unused buildings in a small crossroads settlement.

Old Filling Station
This former filling station is located close to the border, southwest of Newtownhamilton.

Gibbsian Door
Gibbsian door in a church, Mullavilly.

Georgian Door
Located in Loughgall.

Loughgall
The stone building to the left is the former Market House. Built in 1746, the market
was held on the lower floor and the upper floor was used as a courthouse.

The Manor House
Loughgall.

Loughgall Gates
Built in 1842 at a cost of c. £3000 as the entrance to the Manor House.

Dan Winter's Cottage
One of the last houses in Ireland to be made with oak timbers,
constructed in the early eighteenth century.

Right: **Country Scene**
Landscape close to Portadown.

Storm Over Fields
A spring storm.

House and Lake
Disused buildings close to a lake in the east of the county.

Edge of Woods

Edge of natural woodland near Lough Neagh. Prior to widespread deforestation, oak woods were common, hence the many placenames beginning with Derry, Doire in Irish, meaning oak grove.

Bog Cotton
Common throughout Ireland, bog cotton or cottongrass spreads rapidly where conditions allow.
The leaves turn from green to red in autumn, adding to the overall redness of bog landscapes.

Peatlands Park
Path through Peatlands Park. There are 10 miles of paths through the 680 acre site.

Peatlands Park
The peatbog here has been in existence since the end of the Ice Age about 10,000 years ago.

Peatlands Park
The park was set up to promote peatland awareness, and is home to many species of insect, and woodland and wetland birds. Lizards and newts can also be found here.

Right: **River Blackwater**
The western boundary of Armagh, for most of its length, follows the River Blackwater which flows into Lough Neagh at Maghery. Seen here is a Lough Neagh boat, large enough to handle the waves that build up on the lake.

River Bann
The river flows into Lough Neagh a few miles east of Maghery.
It starts in the Mourne Mountains and to the north its lower
course is the only river to flow out of Lough Neagh. This
stretch is very popular for coarse angling.

Left: **Coney Island**
Offshore from Maghery, Coney Island is thickly wooded and
has a history of habitation from the Mesolithic, or 6000 BC.
Situated close to the mouths of the River Blackwater and the
River Bann, it was one of the most westerly Anglo-Norman
outposts in the north c. 1265.

Drumlin Landscape
Near Keady.

Right: **Evening Landscape**
Late evening looking northwards from the Fews area.

Castle Street, Armagh
Also known as Whaley's
Buildings. Built in 1773.

Below: **View from
Cathedral Gardens**
Looking over Castle Street,
the gardens lie inside the
cathedral grounds.

The Mall
In summer the Mall is used by cricketers and picnickers.

Armagh Skyline
View of Armagh from one of its seven hills.

Tassagh Viaduct and Mill
Opened to traffic in 1909, the viaduct has 11 arches and is a very impressive landmark
in Armagh. Constructed from 500,000 bricks it is one of the last great railway structures to be
built in Ireland. In front can be seen a former large beetling mill.

Dundrum House and Gates
These cast iron gates were saved from melting down during the
Second World War; they date from the early nineteenth century.

Mill Ruins
Mill ruins can be found all over Armagh but particularly in the Callan valley.
Linen was the speciality, but paper was also produced.

Mill Ruins, Keady
Situated close to Keady, these mills were established in 1826 by Sadler of Leeds.

Right: **Landscape near Tassagh**
Green countryside close to Tassagh.

View from Darkley
The remains of Darkley Mill to the left, overlooking the valley northwards.

Armaghbreague
The mythological King Lir had his palace in the area close to here.

Armaghbreague
A legend of St Patrick tells that he built his first church in Armaghbreague, but that every night a bull would knock down what he had built. Armaghbreague means 'false Armagh'.

Road Racing
Horse and trap road races are common on the roads south of Armagh.

Abandoned Farmhouse
Evening sunlight on a ruined farmhouse.

Clontygora

Meaning Meadow of the Goats, very little remains of the stone cairn which would have covered this tomb. Despite this, it remains a very impressive site.

Clontygora

The largest orthostats (upright stones) seen here are 2.75m high.

Ballykeel Dolmen
A tripod dolmen, the capstone was reset in position in the 1960s.
The archaeological remains found include decorated pottery, flint and a javelin head.

Ballymacdermot
Dating from around 3500 BC, this cairn is situated on the edge of a steep
slope with sweeping views over the plain of Meigh.

Ross Lake
Summer evening at Lough Ross, Crossmaglen.

115

Annaghmare
The entrance to the gallery of
Annaghmare court tomb.

Right: **Annaghmare
Court Tomb**
The court tomb is quite unusual
as it features large orthostats
with dry stone walling. Located
close to Crossmaglen.

Ring of Gullion
The Ring of Gullion is the best preserved ring dyke in Ireland or Britain, and consists of Slieve Gullion at the centre of a concentric set of lower hills 10km across.

Left: **Ballymacdermot Gallery**
View from inside the gallery of Ballymacdermot.

Gullion Drive
View from the forest and mountain drive on Slieve Gullion.

Fathom Viewpoint
The view south over Warrenpoint and Carlingford. Visible is the Irish Sea, and on the estuary side in
Co. Down can be seen Narrow Water Castle. Fathom is close to the border with Co. Louth.

Hearty's Folk Cottage
A restored thatched cottage, near Glassdrummond in South Armagh contains a traditional pub.

Creggan Church
In the village of Creggan, this church dates from 1731, but stands on a fifteenth-century ecclesiastical site. It was the burial place of the O'Neills from 1480. The graveyard also contains the graves of three eighteenth-century poets.

The Poets' Glen
This glen runs through Creggan and was a haunt of many poets including Art MacCooey who wrote:
'Should I die in some far-off country, in our wanderings east and west,
In the fragrant clay of Creggan let my weary heart have rest.'

124

Gorse
Gorse, also known as whin or furze can be seen all over South Armagh.
A favourite plant of Linnaeus, it adds a golden colour to the landscape.

Ring of Gullion
View over the Ring of Gullion.

Killeavy
These two churches are aligned in a row east-west. The older is ninth century in origin and the other thirteenth century. The site was founded as a convent in the fifth century by St Monenna, also known as St Darerca.

Craigmore Viaduct from Bernish Viewpoint
The Craigmore railway viaduct as seen from Bernish Viewpoint overlooking Newry. The viaduct is the longest and highest in Ireland and consists of 18 arches. It carried its first train in May 1852.

Craigmore Horses
Horses in a meadow in front of Craigmore viaduct. Each of the 18 arches spans
60ft and the highest is 150ft above ground level.

Right: **Rapeseed**
A typical late summer scene in the north and east of the county.

Farming Scene
Summer silage harvesting is dependent on good weather, and harvesting can go on all through the night.

Typical Landscape near Keady
Rolling drumlins characterise
much of Armagh.

Navan Fort Sunset
Atmospheric sunset at Navan Fort.

Right: **Navan Fort**
Navan, along with nearby associated sites, is regarded as the most important
archaeological area in Northern Ireland.

River Callan
Callan River near Tassagh.

Right: **Woodland River**
One of the many rivers
flowing through the county.

Tassagh, River and Bridge
Here the Callan River flows through Tassagh past quiet backroads with wooded riverbanks.

Clare Glen
The Cusher River seen here flowing through Clare Glen, a wooded river valley.

Armagh Gaol
Interior of Armagh Gaol. Designed by Thomas Cooley, dating from 1780 and empty since 1986.
The gaol is currently undergoing a period of public consultation to decide its future.

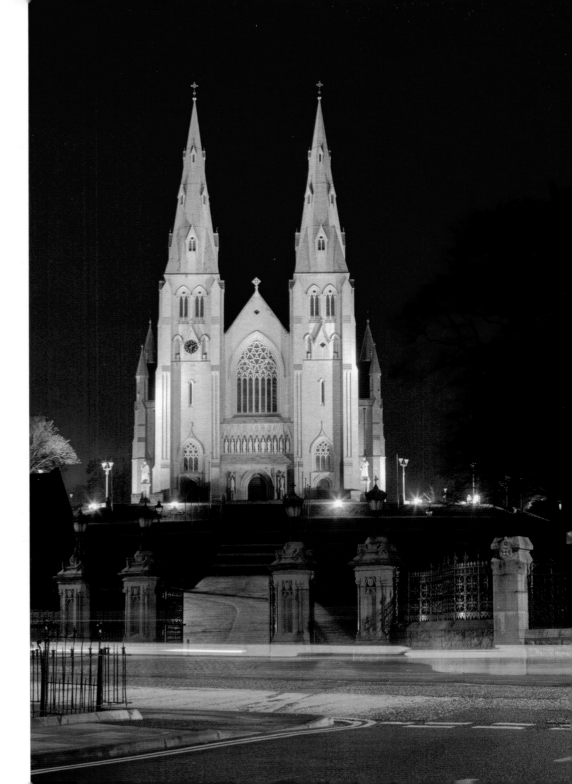

St Patrick's Cathedral
Night view of the
Roman Catholic Cathedral.

143

St Patrick's Church of Ireland Cathedral
Night view of the cathedral.